GRASSHOPPER
GURU

GRASSHOPPER
GURU

Jane Brunette

flamingseed
press

table of contents

ISBN 978-0-9892605-1-0

BOOK DESIGN:
Jane Brunette

PHOTOS:
Grasshopper
by ithinksky

Muddy boots
by Péter Gudella

Two hands open in prayer
by Christopher Meder

PUBLISHED BY:
Flamingseed Press
California

flamingseedpress.com
flamingseed.com

Part 2
How to Pray | 57

To all the wise ones,
strangers, insects and trees
who have received me
with hospitality and taught me
as surely as any guru.

And to my mother
and grandmothers,
who taught me
that however it might appear
at times, this being human
is a love story.

Preface: Muddy sky beneath my feet

AS A CHILD, I WANTED TO BE A SAINT. I thought this meant I had to be good. How strange to learn that my strategy was all wrong. Saints are not conventionally good. They are fierce rebels against a status quo that keeps our fear at bay by starving our souls—the only part of us capable of sainthood. While many use the distractions of the material world to keep their rebel souls from taking charge, I confess that I have often unknowingly used spirituality to accomplish the same thing. When I recognized this, I changed my primary aspiration from sainthood to soulhood, and took as guru the whole of imminent creation, right down to the grasshoppers.

Soul is not a popular word among Buddhists or pragmatists, but I think it ought to be. For me, the soul is where the universal meets the human, where something of our true nature—or the holy spirit, in Christian terms—moves our limbs in a singular way that puts us in harmony with the whole. It seems the essential point of any spiritual practice is to find that place in us so that we can let go of the lonely, fearful, idea that we are separate beings who need to survive on our own and instead become connected instruments for universal compassion.

For me, there is no aspiration more worthy, but invisible assumptions formed by social and cultural conditioning have proven to be formidable obstacles to consistently embodying this. I've found the trance of this prison extremely difficult to

see and release while living inside the walls of American con-
sumer culture, and so for a number of years I have been called
to travel, live simply and do solitary retreat in India, Nepal,
North and South America, Bali and Thailand. This collection
reflects my inner journey as I was held by these landscapes, and
the book as a whole forms a kind of memoir of the wave-like
movement of spirit through my soul as I attempted to see and
transmute layers of personal, ancestral and collective shadow
into compassionate action.

WHILE THE BULK of my spiritual training has been in Tibetan
Buddhism and I feel immense gratitude and connection to that
lineage, my particular path has required that I look through a
number of lenses from varying traditions to break through my
stubborn habits of mind. Given this, it seems most accurate to
claim primary membership in what I call the lineage beyond
lineages, which is reflected in the mystic heart of every spiritual
tradition, and so you will find in this collection references to
God, Buddha, Jesus, Mary, Krishna, Rumi, shamans and the
wisdom imminent in nature. For me, the view from each of
these vantage points has illuminated particular aspects of a
mystery far bigger than any concept.

As a child, I wanted to be a saint and thought it was a special calling. Now it seems to me that we are all called to make
our home among the communion of saints by becoming soulful
humans in love with the whole, using whatever means will as-
sist us. Life is becoming aware of itself and this mystery can't
be contained—it spills out of all our boxes into a vast ground
of openness and benevolence far beyond what our limited
human minds can conceive.

Jane Brunette
Bali, Indonesia
February 2013

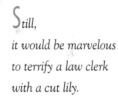

Still,
it would be marvelous
to terrify a law clerk
with a cut lily.

—PABLO NERUDA

FEET ON
THE EARTH,
ARMS
INTO SPACE

Grasshopper Guru

I left the stormy city traffic for a house made of dry mud and that who for three days spoke truth from the kitchen wall left through the open window, then came back to make one more point about the necessity of idleness.

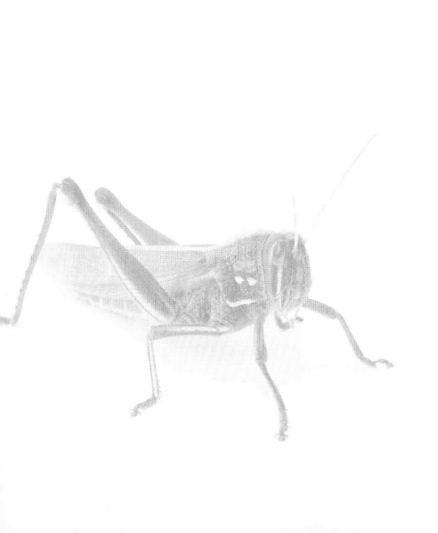

DRUNKEN FLOWERS

Under the mask I wear
or you wear
or we take off and leave
like drunken flowers
at the side of the road,
a face not yet exposed to sunlight—
the texture of a hydrangea petal
before its edges go brown.

I want to put my finger there,
see if I can sense the echo of birth
and the bright sky we fell from,
sunlight skimming
over the tree canopy
as we slid down
into the heavy atmosphere of earth,
masks forming as we fell

like angels
growing lobster shells.

IN A PLACE WHERE TREES CAN SPEAK

Andes Mountains, Ecuador

Everywhere, trees can speak
but not everywhere can I listen.

In this glade
kept safe from crowbars and chain saws,
I lean my head into the wilco's[1] bark—
feel it breathe with me.

When the trees have been sent away
they don't easily return.
And the ocelet who lay on the branch
goes with them.

I swing from the limb
of my grandfather's apple tree.
Blossoms scatter;
the wind takes their petals.
Even in memory, the trees give.

[1] *Sacred tree indigenous to Ecuador and Peru*

WE CALL IT A FLOOR

Before me at my feet,
the wood of an oak that dwelled in a forest.
A nest of blue jays lived in its hair.
Now we call it a floor.
Once it was an acorn,
or a shoot off the root of its mother.
Once it lived in open sky
as the earth tumbled through vastness.
Then someone came with a saw and cut.
End of "tree."
Beginning of "floor."
The Saw Maker dreamed
this flattened oak
would hold a being
who writes words in a book
made from other trees
now pressed into thin layers
that will turn brittle with time
and crumble to dust.

STILL BEHIND YOU ON THE FREEWAY

Andes Mountains, Ecuador

Once, I lived next to the freeway
and watched a human stream—
the sound it made like water
surging over boulders.

Now, in a remote cabin,
I listen to the river
in the valley below
growl like a dishwasher

and that strange squeak is back
from the bug I can't find,
metal on metal,
like the faulty brakes of an oil truck.

SHORELINE

The moon never left today,
just stayed smeared over the world.
Night and day not so different as they seem.

Now that time has melted,
I see the agreement we made
to slice eternity into decimals
is convenient
but has no particular reality.

In the melting world,
we are the shoreline
between dark and light,
body and sky.

THE LAST FLIGHT OF THE FIELD MOUSE

Andes Mountains, Ecuador

The rickety tree house
where I sit,
watching the light shift
on the wall of mountains
across the gorge,
could be an eagle's nest.

Something makes me want to jump,
feel nubs in my back
stretch out into wings.

And I remember
the last flight of the field mouse:
how the hawk swooped
and scooped him up—
so close,
just a few feet in front of me.

I could hear that mouse squeal
and called to him to relax.
Just once
in the hawk's claw
that mouse could fly.

SO TINY

I listen for the guru:
in a cricket,
in the wings of a blue dragonfly
whirring up through the pines,
in the murmur of mantra
from a drumming heart.

Perhaps in the dry grass,
its golden whispers
to the wind,
or in the tree frog's croak
from the outdoor sink—
so tiny.

I listen into the space
between my cells,
where the Buddhas
lay their eggs of light.
The dark had its day:
humility and the treacherous.

Now something rests
at the base of my lineage tree,
without dorje, talisman
or crucifix—
no rattle, no hymn,
no thighbone trumpet:

A caterpillar, silent,
belly to the earth,
sure it knows who it is.
Tomorrow
it will melt into wings—
move to the sky.

HOLY RELICS

I exist because of the European lust
for drafty castles and beaver pelts
such that they killed all their beavers
and my French grandfathers crossed an ocean
to hunt the northern forests
peopled by tribes who don't go in for castles—
just the sky and winter long houses.

Those adventurous men found home
in the arms of my tribal grandmothers.
When they died, their bones
tangled with tree roots
nestled in black earth.

By the time I was born,
castle mind had taken root
along with the lust for things
that kill forests.
But the trees never let me enjoy
the dead world of shiny things.

I came to life in the White Mountains
when I slept on a ridge with a mountain lion.
There, I found a rock with a name
and the pelvis of a weasel
bleached by the sun.

Later, I visited the Holy Man.
Behind earnest yogis holding statues of deities
I stood in line with that bone
to have it blessed.

He asked, "What is this?"
"A pelvis," I answered.

What else was there to say?

ONCE I FELT THE BREATH OF GOD

Once I felt the breath of God
waft from a small hole in the bare earth
near Harney Peak.[1]

I put my palm above the hole
reverent as prayer
and wonder.

A woman appeared from the parking lot,
shoved her palm beneath mine.
"That's weird," she said

and left to find
a hot dog stand.

[1] *A mountain peak located in the Black Hills of South Dakota
and considered sacred by the Lakota people.*

TIPS FOR RE-ENCHANTMENT

The magic hides
from those in a hurry—
those without respect
for black ants on a mottled tile floor.
So much stays hidden
without an attitude of offering.

I give my eyes to the blindness,
that it might see ants for the first time.
I give my ears to the deafness
that it might hear an echo
from the dense, tangled forest
where macaws screech,
flash their color through the canopy.

We humans seldom leave our species
to look for gurus
and this might be the trouble.
What is the grammar
of a white river dolphin
glowing pink from blood
flowing in red rivers
beneath translucent skin?

LONELY FOR DARKNESS

I get lonely for darkness, for shadows
that melt daylight into riddle.

I want the cover of twilight fog
where deer emerge as dream animals.

Dark, like the mud in the lotus pond
where frogs are born.

We avoid it with electric lights,
piped-in dreams—dubious comfort.

The measure of stillness
is how alone with the sky I can be

even when low grumbling from the blackness
could be rats or an untamed fury.

When the night is over,
the sun comes up without me asking.

THAT STRANGE BEE

Forgotten dreams
curdle in my stomach
like undigested meat,
while the breeze that would heal
stays trapped between tongue
and collarbone.

My breath wants to make
a break for the wind—
follow that strange bee
with its wooly orange body,
black legs dangling,
wobbly as noodles.

If the route of his flight
lacerated the sky,
would heaven fall through?
Or would I finally see
the torn edge of canvas
that proves this world
a stage set?

I PUT A HOLE IN THE SKY

The world depends on me
attending to what is small.
Busy with significance,
I bought take out
and threw away the packaging.

I forgot my water bottle,
got thirsty, bought a plastic one.
Because isn't that just a detail?
Tiny, compared to the real problems
out there, that *they* need to fix?

I know the truth now.
There are no small transgressions.

My heedless bottle
is the stench of burning plastic.
It is the oil spill in the Gulf,
children with birth defects
on the banks of the Amazon,
Fukishima,
the hole in the sky.

THE IDEA THAT MADE ME

This mindscape:
a tangle of trapezes
that keeps me from putting
feet on the earth,
arms into space.

And yet,

the idea that ideas
can hold me tight—
like a grizzly or a lover—
is only just
another
idea.

WITHOUT FEATHERS

We live in animal bodies
and sometimes they whimper.
Part of the experience here.

I am without feathers.
My body calls me inside:
only this will make me transparent.

Otherwise, my cells are little bricks
with cracked mortar.
A crumbling building of self.

I stumble through the sacred,
not wanting advice.

WHAT IS OVER BUT STILL LOVED

Andes Mountains, Ecuador

What is over but still loved
comes to me like a fish under the algae,
breaking its soft surface,
the pond coated in green fur
and now cut with the lines of the fish—

cut like a wound from a knife blade
or the sudden line from an artist's pen
sure of its way even as it sinks
into dark water.

What is over but still loved
arrives in vague dreams
like the drift of clouds that gather
at the mountain's peak
between the fists of Mandango[1]
where the bandits hide with their machetes

and tiny white flowers spin upward
on their rickety stems.
Do they exist
or do I dream they exist?
So much they resemble
the five-petal drawings of a child.

[1] *The peak of a sacred mountain in Southern Ecuador
that resembles a reclining warrior.*

Everything is over as soon as it is born
and carries a fragrance,
like the white jasmine that swayed in the breeze
outside the kitchen window — painted shut:

I could see the blossoms
but not smell them.

WON'T LET GO

Andes Mountains, Ecuador

I have been a weasel in my dark hole,
the cabin fogged in, damp.
Something in me hangs on with all my teeth
to a bone I don't even want to chew.

I'd like to tame my inner weasel
but I hear they are dangerous,
crazy little beings
with a grip that won't let go.

PERFECT MUDRAS

I saw a butterfly with a torn wing.
And that butterfly could still fly.
It made me want to paint a Buddha
with a leper's stunted fingers,
making mudras.

I think of the party
at the Benares Leper colony.
The old man's unabashed joy—
shaking his hips to Krishna,
stamping his club foot.

WHEN THE SKY OWNS ME

I lie on the earth
like a grape
on an offering tray.
The sky opens its mouth
and eats.
No napkin. No tea cup.

Now, I am the mouse
in the hawk's claw.
I am that strange feather
carried on the wind to the field.
I forget my name,
what country I'm in.

The morning comes
and those roosters
could be anywhere.
The sky doesn't care.
It is everywhere at once.
And when the sky owns me,
so am I.

THIS IS NOT A TRAGEDY

This is not a tragedy—
though everywhere, motors blare,
tearing things from the earth
without asking permission.

It only looks like a tragedy
when I think I know better than life
where this labyrinth ought to go.

The dark can't stand up to the fearless love
of a tender, foolhardy adventurer
enjoying every finch and thistle on the hillside

even as the city
threatens to swallow that hillside,
those thistles, those finches.

Later,
the earth will swallow the city
as it has swallowed so many before.

This is not a tragedy—
but an invitation
to jump into the maddening riddle
of hot and cold.

RUNNING WATER IS OPTIONAL

What does it mean when we only embrace
what makes us comfortable?
How will we learn that buckets have souls?

My bucket baths in the Bengali village:
I washed one limb at a time
with attention that a shower won't afford
and then the faintness of life disappeared
into ecstasy
under a solid sheet of water.

Try it sometime.

SOMEONE PUT YOU THERE

I had a talk
with a potted plant today.
Who knows why that came up?

But I touched its wooly leaf and said:
You're lucky.
You don't need to decide where to go.
Someone put you there.

The plant answered:
You are the same.
Someone put you there.

And I was startled.
Am I as choiceless as a potted plant?
And then what is my job?

Just to be, as the plant just is.
Leave the rest to the Gardener.

WINGS

I confess:
I don't want to live
a steady existence
behind sheer living room curtains.
I lose the life signal and start to fade.

Again and again,
I throw off what stifles
and immediately lunge
for a new piece of ground,
same as the old.

Could we give up our clenching?
Hook into nothing
but the sky and the moment?
Maybe the whole world would unravel
and no one would go to work in the morning.

We'd all be outside
with the droning bees,
following the call
of a migrating bird
perched too high in the tree
for us to glimpse

her wings.

WHERE HOME LIVES

Home used to live near a porch
where I befriended the ants
on the round buds of peonies
as storm clouds gathered
over white birch.

Then home lived in a landscape
with rocks that I named,
a moss-covered redwood that carried my thumbprint,
a crevice in the footpath
that became a stream in spring.

The place I called home
could have been lost
but instead hid inside
like a sprout or a seedpod
waiting to be planted in new ground.

Now home lives beneath my feet
anywhere the plants grow vivid with presence
and I forget to remember
what I think I want—
what with the now
taking up all the space.

STRANGE KITTEN

In the wild edges of mind
windswept and thick with undergrowth
I might find a strange kitten
unafraid to pad through the vines
that can tangle and trap—
meeting all with curious play.
I, on the other hand, fear the dark edges
and look for a lit candle
or a path cut for me
by benevolence.

If my feet were full of light,
each step would make the trail
through new territory
but my heart stumbles on the line
between hope and fear.
The dead world beckons
with promise of security—
a sameness that dulls me to trance
even while inside
a lion paces,
ready for new territory.

OFFERINGS

Andes Mountains, Ecuador

I once wandered the open spaces
of North Dakota
until the Black Hills came into view.

Now, I remember only that field of sunflowers
in the night, how the heat lightening
burst their howling yellow from the blackness.

My time in the wooden cabin
leaves no footprints
as I wander these latent landscapes

complete with tangerine tree
and the bat who ate them under the shingles
dropping the peels through a hole in the roof

to land on my altar
as offerings.

SURPRISED BY WINGS

Birth is something
I've witnessed only once.

A cocoon shook and rumbled,
then cracked.

A large black bug emerged
all pointy knees and elbows.

It danced a strange, frightened fury.
The movement dried it off.

Sudden creamy wings unfurled
like sails on a ship—

then the fingers of the wind
lifted it to the sky.

FERAL CHILDREN

Wild jungle girl.
Naked human animal.
Took my lunch.
Catch that girl.
Nabbed at 27.

She's not alone.
A Siberian boy.
Careful, he bites.
Raised by dogs.
Found at 7.

John of Uganda.
To the forest.
New family there.
African grey monkeys.
Discovered at 6.

Ramu of Luknow.
Raised by wolves.
Chews his bones.
Laps his milk.
Returned at 7.

Angel of Nairobi.
Abandoned in forest.
Found by dog.
Joined puppy litter.
Discovered by owner.

Now in captivity.

THE YEAR I HATED BUILDINGS

Wandering spirit imprisoned
since the wild places
were hacked, tamed and eaten
by the hungry comfortable.

Secret caves where mystics
took shelter—exposed.
Primordial forests—
thinned, anemic.

In love with the ancient
and the doomed,
I long for a forest commons,
an outdated hospitality

inviting pilgrims:
refugees from creeping industry,
from this electric world.

NEW STORY

Los Encantos, Ecuador

A new story writes itself
if I follow the urge that comes
from a different place in the body—
not the head that already knows
but the pull in the belly
without ideas to warp it.

Then life leaves the realm of genre
and enters the space
between yes and no—
enjoying the thick smell of clothing
exposed to wind, air, heat and mud.

I folded my dirty clothes
there on the shaman's porch,
all judgments washed away
by fire and moon,
and the stench became music
in the square ponds of cities.

STOPOVER IN SINGAPORE

I miss the dark forest
where the music of night
brings me in and down
to where original story was born.

I want Singapore to go black,
crumble into the ocean's mouth
and from the rubble,
the earth can sculpt a new island
free of glamorous death by concrete.

Could we welcome the redemption
of true night
blanketing neon shopping centers?

This is not a dream:
Under the Victoria's Secret store,
the skulls of the forgotten ones whisper,
preserved in an air-tight spot
for the ones who need to find them.

LIFE IN THE OPEN AIR

Bali, Indonesia

The rain and the water from the faucet
know each other well
though one has just plunged from the clouds.

My pillows were plucked from ducks
and wrapped with woven fibers
in a village exempt from time.

Three moths birthed themselves
on the potted palm at the edge of my porch,
swayed like ivory sailboats

on broken cocoons.

HERE, NOW

Bali, Indonesia

The monitor lizard
padding across the muddy rice field
lifts its snake head
not just to catch a snack with its tongue,
but to deliver a message:
there is no such thing as ordinary.

Without the burden of hope
this moment opens wide and stretches,
happy to be just as it is
here and now,
rain on the pond
and a rice farmer, undaunted.

PERFECTLY RIPE

Andes Mountains, Ecuador

The mango falls into my hand,
the tangerines to the stone walkway
that leads to the cabin.
So many tangerines
there for the bats.

But I open the avocado too soon.

Life ripens
at its own pace
and won't be hurried.

Outside the kitchen window
green bananas hang in the sky
clustered above their lurid red pod—
perfectly ripe
for what they are doing
right now.

FALLOW

I don't know where to place myself.
Everything fell away.
I thought God would step in,
show me what was next.
But I just keep waiting.
Past due.

The only thing that soothes now
is to walk on the earth.
Naked wild land and wind,
hawks over the hilltops—
there, in silence,
something makes sense.

I want to lay still
until God moves me
or die waiting.

I CAN'T KNOW THE NEXT WORD

Unfettered.
Drift of wind through me.
Forget what the future said.
Eyes closed, I can't know the next word.
Let the hands speak.
Only the hands.

Below:
the ancestors bones.
Above:
green leaves, wings.

I dissolve,
trust the arms of mother sky.
Life comes by itself—
moves my limbs without help of the mind.

The scent of fennel drifts in through the window.
On the hillside, thistles go dry.

It's okay that I won't survive.

THE VIEW FROM THE SKY

We emerge from the tunnel wet
naked
learning to scream—
the string to another world cut
and immediately we are taught
to wrap ourselves
against the sharp teeth of the sky
we swim in.

The sky is not a painted ceiling.
We live in the sky—
whirl through it
on a watery ball.

We live in the sky
and the sky lives in us—
even here
on a white plastic chair,
roosters singing their afternoon prayers—
this is the view from the sky.

Really, we've been tromping through clouds
the whole time
our feet seemed to sink into mud.
I wonder at how thick
those clouds can feel
as I scrape them
from my boots.

2

IN DARK WATER,
SHADOWS LINGER

How to Pray: Hide under a blanket with the real and tell everything. Empty your insides. Say out loud those damp things in the shadows. Dry them in the sun——then decide what to keep.

SOMETIMES WE TOUCH

Sometimes we touch each other's fingers
without noticing how strange
that there are fingers at all.

Sometimes we touch the holy
and call it mud
or dust, or grass clippings.

Sometimes we touch the sacred
in the darkened city streets
with a security guard watching.

Sometimes the sacred touches us
in the breeze from a hummingbird's wings
just before the river leaves its banks.

I am in a house
floating in water
thinking of the pocketbooks
the grandmothers carried.

SOLAR ECLIPSE

Darkness nourishes seed and fetus.
Under black sky, things happen.
I can't know what.

Something to do with birth
and the treachery of shadows—
the whispering spirits
who live in dusty shoe boxes
in my mother's attic.

They send their familiars in the night
to churn my dreams
with the distress of frayed lineage.

I saw a void as I fell asleep.
A luminous escalator appeared.
Why an escalator?

Why the black velvet painting
of a street lamp
over my aunt's electric fireplace?

Children know—
they revere both sun and lamp post
astounded
that either exists at all.

HIDDEN CLUES

Himalayan Mountains, India

I wake to the sound of sadhana
sung by monks in their red shawls—
invoking Mahakala.[1]
The master of that temple
visits me in the night
leaving clues in hidden places.

To find them,
I must pass by the obvious—
move as a lion,
stealthy,
to the ragged beginnings
of ecstasy:

Lips shudder to speak
from a lesion in the heart—
last gasp of the grieved child.
What is gone but not forgotten
still rises like steam
from the crack between worlds.

In a Himalayan valley
too remote for bandits and tourists,
someone drags a bundle with a knotted rope
to feed the wise one in her shack—
water dripping,
the kettle cold.

---

[1] *Fierce protector diety from Vajrayana Buddhism.*

WHERE IT ALL STARTED

My life began in a forest
where the trees,
hungry for communion, breathed out
so my ancient mother could breathe in,
belly swollen with the light
of another ancestor
who lived before the ground opened
and sprung an excess of thought.

Later, a womb
where a tiny being with a tail
swam toward an orb of light.
I watched from somewhere nowhere
and saw a universe I wanted to swallow,
even with all its bitterness and fear.

Then I lay in a hospital
tiny fists at my ears
and the face
that could have been from anywhere.
I had just been a fish, a lizard
and a bird. I had just emerged
from liquid God,
water infused with light.

I came in through my mother,
who lent me her genes,
her belly and blood
long enough to make a "me"
who would learn to see this gift
as so precious and strange,
all else could be forgiven.

BEGINNING AT THE END

After reading Annie Dillard, as the Gulf filled with oil

In the beginning, God spread curiosity
all through the sky.

We put the world in our mouths,
curious, the way I drank that glass of turpentine
next to my brother's oil paints
because it looked like chocolate milk.
Outside, the cloud's reflection in a sidewalk puddle
might have been the sky of a lower world.
If I stepped in, I'd fall as Alice fell
and no ladder could bring me back.

In the beginning, God appeared in a garden
and dared us not to eat
but we ate for the sake of curiosity,
wanting to know,
to leave the garden for the alleyways
where broken glass shimmers like spring puddles.

During the violence,
can anyone still feel the connection
that runs deeper than surface aggression?
Then the body rules. Ears twitch
just before the deer feels teeth on her neck.

The heroic ones keep their backbone.
As the rabbi was tortured, he said his prayers
because it was time to say them.
Torture couldn't keep him from his God.

In the beginning, God used no calculators.
The fecundity of wild play.
Mass proliferation. Mass extinction.

Every few minutes, another pelican
pulls itself from the oily water,
feathers heavy,
soaked in rusty film the color of blood.
In 400 years, all the species we know will be dead.
There have been massive die-offs before.
Then spring comes
and a seed pushes a stem up through the earth.

In the lava fields,
people bring tiny coconut sprouts
and plant them in the cracks.

IN THE WITCH'S GARDEN

Los Encantos, Ecuador

In the witch's garden
where the San Pedro cactus grew,
I saw the past as a pile of broken things.
My brother's wooden giraffe,
my grandfather's rusty nails
in old baby food jars,
emerged from the compost of earth.

I've had hauntings.
Spirits cling to me
when I let down my guard.
They murmur inside.
I have thoughts that aren't mine.
But maybe no thoughts
belong to a thinker.

We are composite beings
made from what came before
and our hearts are portals
that take us back.
My grandfather's pocket watch:
I go inside it,
hear the ticking.

MY GRANDMOTHER WENT TO THAT SCHOOL

Menominee Nation, Wisconsin

As a girl, she whispered in her native tongue
and was tortured for it
in the government boarding school.

The Menominee man told me
how the other girls were forced by the nuns
to pour boiling water on his grandmother's back.
Age 92, and she still has the welts.

I sat with him on a wooden bench
in a tribal school room
and didn't brush the tears away.
They left streaks on my face,
dripped fire from my chin:

This grief I used to run from,
not knowing it was the way home.

Later, I saw a kitten with a crushed tail
and still she found her balance,
her injury defining her
just as the sharp edges of history
define me

as a human soul,
touched by the infinite
in the places that hurt.

SOMEWHERE, EYES WATCH EVERYTHING

Big Island, Hawaii

In a Hawaiian hut
I drifted through the rafters—
a fever cloud in a landscape of sound:
the trill of a bird I never saw,
a steady roar that told me of ocean,
passing cars like thunder clouds.
Between layers of time, I was, and the spirits
entered me there—fever, their doorway.

Before I had a chance to look
they used my eyes to see.
People tell me Hawaii is paradise
but when the fever broke,
I saw only home invasion.
The burglars never left.

Another culture unravels, like the frayed edge
of my grandmother's tatted tablecloth
hanging low on the polished wood.
She wet the thread with her own saliva
to get it through the needle's hole.
I wonder if she learned to tat lace
at the government boarding school
where she lived without mother or tribe?

During the violent hour,
when the power that explodes volcanos
surges through human collectives,
nothing to do but hold fast,
feet firm on the foot path
that stretches upward into jagged peaks
where new varieties of love are born
from the same chaos that made continents.

UNFINISHED WORLD

At estate sales,
I am touched by the craft kits, undone,
patches for quilts never made.
We can leave our projects:
Not everything started
must be completed.

If I were to walk this unfinished world
without the belief that things
ought to complete themselves,
I might enter a slow dance with life,
leave the threshold between now and then.

Instead,
I lie with head in the lap of my own sadness
until I want to kiss the fingers of every hand
that lay limp on a breakfast table,
the seed of compassion still germinating
from the night, long and cold.

STIGMATA

I step onto the blacktop roof
of a drab cement building
where a little girl sits, placid,
under somber sky.
Sunlight leaks
through a crack in the grey air,
licks her foot.
A brilliant prism of color appears—
forms a mandala on the water tank.

I take a step toward her
and see the mandala is made
of colored glass shards
wedged into the tender skin
of her little foot,
blood still seaping
from the sharpest corners.

Pain turned to beauty.

Awe ruptures my heart
and I kiss her holy foot.
Then, fear speaks:
What if someone is watching,
furious
that I didn't remove the glass?

What would I say?

AT THE WINDOW

Outside the window, I think I see a face.
This happens at dusk:
someone comes through in shadow's light
from the other world where the ancestors live.
Did I really see it?
The elders say we only eat and breathe
so this body can dream.
All the important things happen
with eyes veiled by darkness,
moon pointing to truth.
In the morning,
the world presses against the window glass.
A thin film of curtain
can't keep it at bay.

SETTLERS AND SAINTS

1.
On a narrow street
in front of an ancient library,
a hollow-cheeked man arranges
tooled leather books
in arcane German,
yellowed pages crumbling.

"These books are rare and precious," I say.
"Why do you sell them for pennies
on the street?"

"No one reads them anymore,"
he tells me. "We need room
on the shelves for the new."

Dismayed, I buy what I can carry.

2.
My father's face appears
in the sky
like the vision of a deity,
a single tear on one cheek.

"You don't know
where I come from," he says.

I wake up, determined to find out.

3.

In the village of Marpingen
where his grandmother's family lived,
a crackdown on "superstition,"
reforming witches and priests,
mystics and dreamers.
Then a young girl
had a vision of Mother Mary
near a spring in a forest knoll.

She was weeping.
Mother Mary always weeps.
Scent of roses,
white robes floating
in a tender, open sky.
Her message was love.
Her message is always love.

Throngs of pilgrims
surged into the village
singing Marian hymns—
stripping bark from the trees
as talismans
amidst miracles, cures, omens.

A ban on public devotion:
Divine apparations
now enemies of progress.
The visionary captured,
caged in an orphanage.
Villagers detained
for taking in pilgrims,
aiding the priests.

Still, my great grandmother
answered a knock at the door,
offered a pilgrim
a bed and a meal.
In the morning,
she sent her son, Nicholaus,
to open the church,
ring the bell.

A large crowd gathered
for the criminal Mass,
with Nicholaus serving
as altar boy. Soldiers burst in
and the pilgrim—now priest—
cast off his robe
revealing outlawed prince
and bishop.

Wielding a broom,
my tiny great grandmother
thrashed the soldiers
at the door of her kitchen—
come to take everything
that fed them.

Boys drafted—
so the family fled for America
to keep another generation from dying
in a bloody Alsatian war.
They took a chance at peace
in a Midwestern settlement
on land already stolen
from my mother's tribe.

4.
My father came from peasant farmers
and dance-hall musicians,
tailors, merchants,
and classical composers.
They hid Jews in that family
from pogroms and poverty.
They hid mystics and lovers
and fiery women
who defied the new order
to preserve what was precious.

His mother, the mystic,
prayed to St Therése
and the roses bloomed in January.
An image of the Little Flower[1]
hung on his office wall.

[1] *Saint Therese of Liseaux is known as "The Little Flower of Jesus."*
My grandmother often prayed to her, and asked that she send a rose
as a sign that the prayer was heard.

BEHIND THE BIG SMILE

Behind the big smile
in the dark
he lies face down on the bed—
numb, crusty, afraid of the wet,
afraid of the mud,
afraid of the warm mess of life.

I want to tell him:
the invisible holds you like a baby bird
under the warm haunches of a hen,
feathers soft on your cheek.
Put down your gun and your fist.
Put down the knife and the sharp pen.

You can melt now, into warm bread
and bury your face in the safety
of a world birthing love.
The darkness you see:
Just the images
printed on a little boy's bed sheets.

PLEASE DON'T APOLOGIZE

Please don't apologize when the mask slips
and exposes your real face,
naked and absurd.
Ignore the man behind the curtain,
you roar, and immediately, we look closer:
He's the one we came to meet.

Please don't apologize for living as a human—
or forgetting to live.
Let me serve you tea and cookies,
buttery ones with raspberry filling,
and we'll have a talk right here
at the entrance to the underworld—
decide whether to go up or down.

Either way works. Either way an adventure.
(Unless we get all caught up in fantasy
and fall asleep in front of the TV.)

HOLY MADNESS

They say a baby rattlesnake
is the most dangerous of all.

I bit a girl at age 4.
We were going to play hairdresser
and I wanted her to be customer.
After all, I had procured
the forbidden sewing scissors.

She snatched them away
so I sunk my teeth into her forearm
until she howled,
dropped the scissors
and ran home.

Her mother assumed by her wail
that she'd been bitten by a dog
and took her to the hospital
for a series of painful rabies shots.

I was never punished.
She never told.
We never did play hairdresser.
I never atoned.

Now, In the underground cave
where Jesus left his cliff notes,
I bring my neck to Dracula's table
long enough to remember
the gold
hidden inside every obsession.

IS THAT RAT EVER SATISFIED?

The itch moves over my skin
the way it moves through my mind:
The thought that can never be
scratched or caught,
possessed or solved.

Like the rat who comes into
the kitchen at night,
eats the bananas,
then finds a lump of cheese
stuck to the pizza box.

Creation came from a primordial itch—
the kind that finally lands
in the center of my back
where only the hand of another
can reach.

In my medicine bag
is an arrowhead:
I stab my own dark hunger
and offer it to the deity
for breakfast.

FALLEN ANGELS

The oceans are filled with fallen angels—
some of whom perform underwater rituals.

I met a fighter pilot who dropped bombs each week,
then flew to remote corners on his days off to dive.

"I don't know if you've met one of these characters
before," he said, "who kills for a living."

They called him Shark.

He watched a shark devour his diving partner,
leg floating free and ghastly, water turned to wine.

A dark angel's meal.

(We are not so horrified when a fish is eaten,
and assume it less dear to its friends.)

After that, he went in search of shark-infested waters.
Paddled out. Dove in. Faced them off.

How does it feel on the inside, to meet a shark,
to stare him down until he swims away?

"Ice cold," he told me.

Then he filled a bowl with warm milk
for the stray cat.

TODAY I WOULD RATHER SING

I am a cracked doll
slashed open by the night—
sawdust spilled on the floor
from a torn chest cavity,
porcelein feet dangling.

I find a spot on a pink mattress
somewhere on an island
floating in the ocean.
This will have to do, though
what I long for has transparency,
veils of nothing.

Words float
like debris on the pond.
The room that is to be mine
remains empty.
I can only sit on this mattress
and let go of pictures.

At dawn I remember:
The birds rise each morning and sing,
whatever happened in the night.

THE NEXT NEW FRAIL THING

Chicago, Illinois

I lost a brick wall.
Last, I saw it
holding up a bedroom
where the ants crawled.
Those bricks were sewn
from the frail thread
that dissolves all things
into memory.

I lost the yard
where the family picnicked.
While the grill
was heating up,
I turned my eyes to heaven
and flew
until the lovesick song
of the earth
grew too tender to ignore.

I land again.
Their hair is grey.
The babies are tall
and articulate,
driving cars
and dialing phones,

pregnant
with the next
new
frail
thing.

This me:
a bramble of habits
sticky with stubborn lies.

A child emerges
from the blackberry bushes,
fine red lines
etch arms and legs,
face stained purple
to match her hands.

Stung by joy.

FAMILY INHERITANCE

The luminous thighbone of Saint Francis
got passed down in my family
like a Victorian mirror,
the view from a window,
grace said before dinner.
My eldest brother
looks at me from where he crouches,
wrench in one hand,
seed in the other:
"I thought you knew."

I MAKE THE PAST

The ancestors have a gift for me:
lost wisdom and connection.
I have a gift for them:
A cradle for the pain story.

Their world continues in me.
Why pretend a blank slate?
No human is given that.
The past is alive.

The ancestors gather and whisper:
maybe this will be the one
who will heal the lineage story,
write the chapter

that gives it all meaning,
puts it to rest.
Until then, a gap.
Something incomplete.

How I gloss over
the seams I make in history
pretending it wasn't me
who did the stitching.

Now it's my turn
to make the future
with the new past I forge
in every living now.

COMPASSION'S THRONE IS FOR EVERYONE

I stand in the Dalai Lama's room.
In the entry is a throne
meant only for him.
I am tempted to climb onto it,
to see how the world looks from there.

A guard enters, startles me.
What are you doing in here?
Do you dare think
you can step onto that throne?

The Dalai Lama enters
jovial as ever,
puts his hand on the guard's arm.
No problem, no problem,
he says, then turns to me:

Please, please, climb onto that throne.
I would like nothing more
than for you to sit there.

The guard's face goes red.
The Dalai Lama strokes his arm.
And you too, he says.
Just as soon as she's done.
You too.

THE WIND HOLDS THE BUTTERFLY

For Judy

A girl at sixty-five
with a checkerboard brand on her leg--
a medical mistake. I befriended her death
before she did, curled my fingers
around its firm hand;
said yes to letting go.

A dreaming Buddha remembers a temple
crushed by a fallen tree.
I gave her a Buddha head
(kept the body for myself)—
less troubling to her than Jesus.
I gave her my life in a medicine bag

adding a faded picture
of the way she wanted to
be remembered.
Her painting in the hallway
she named, "The Wind
Holds the Butterfly."

Her swollen feet,
too big now for socks.
I touched my palms to her soles
and let her hate me for living.
She cursed me for holding back
on the morphine, though she'd asked,
to give her time to rage.

She promised to come back as the wind
and did, blowing the papers from my desk
in a swirl of fluttering angels;
ringing the chimes I never heard
until the sky
asked for her hand.

TAKE THE STAIRS

The way to
  enlightenment:
    begin on what-
      ever landing you
        find yourself and
          start going down.
            When you run out
              of handrail, hold on
                to your ear. Listen
                  for the place
                      where the whole
                        game seems to
                      reverse and down
                  goes up as the light
                gets dim and the
              basement sends
            its dank smell
          to mingle with
        holy oil until
cold is hot and
  hot is cold and
    the way to truth
      stands still and
        you take another
          step and you enter
                  the

          sky.

A RECENT HISTORY OF WIND

For Hunter

Is the wind made by the blades of a fan?
Or does it just agree to dance,
whirling its finger on your cheek
as you sit, chin in palm,
wondering what to say about your life
and what photo
best pretends a solid self
that you can put your breath in—
wind that you are.

WOULD YOU BE MY GURU?

In a world where peacocks forget to preen,
we will have too many untrained accordion players
so please—sit up straight.
Break open the concrete.
Change your name if you have to.
Just revive the place inside
that knows something about beauty.

We follow what we see and love.
We need examples.
Please, free yourself.
Under the grip of a grey sky,
we can forget how much power our joy has.
The world needs us to love what we love.

If we were to do that with real consistency—
love not what we should love,
but what we actually love—
we'd attract some crazy looking angels
with lion tails and parrot wings.

ALWAYS SO MUCH TOUGHER

Always so much tougher,
to begin
than to be in the middle.
And to be in the middle
than to be at the end.
And to be at the end.

Always so much tougher,
to remember how things change—
how the same four walls
can feel one day like prison,
the next like the key to liberation.

Every mood feels real,
as though I could build a house from it.
Or maybe the house is already built
and I am rattling padlocks
made of dust and air.

WILLING TO BLEED

Quito, Ecuador

1.
In the only church I find unlocked,
the nuns sing blessings for each nation
as Jesus sits wrapped in a green robe
with a shiny white collar. Blood drips
from the corners of his mouth
smearing mustache into beard.
A large wound dominates one cheek.
A brass staff protrudes from his robe.
He seems to have no legs.
Protected by a glass box
lit with two fluorescent tubes,
he lives in a two-story, gold-plated altar.
Candles burn.

I sit in a wooden pew.
Something shakes in me.
Here is the promise:
the suffering has meaning.
You can love through pain.
You can love most sublimely through pain.
Relief, to see a God willing to suffer.
Easy, I think, to be a Buddha
floating in blissful golden light,
sending waves of compassion
to far-off suffering beings.
But down on the ground
it is Jesus who is willing to bleed.

2.

In the airport
a swarm of missionaries arrive
wearing dark suits,
pressed shirts, colorful ties,
hair cropped short like the army.
Faces barely passed the pimple stage
yet their name tags read "Elder."
I'm afraid for someone.
The dangerous innocence of our missions:
We think we know what will help.

Who could argue with my mission:
I want to balance the world.
But can't I see?
I am most balanced when imitating death.
The Creative works by being off-kilter.
Life requires flying—and diving.
My sobriety?
Just another extreme.

The temporary truth:
I look for open moments
and drink the nectar while its fresh.
The rest of the time I spend
in the hallway between simple pleasures.

Sometimes
willing or not
I bleed.

LANGUAGE OF LINEAGE

Our ancestors live in us,
in their lingering sentences,
the pointy handwriting on recipe cards
long ago composted in the field
behind the farmhouse,
feeding asters that tangle
in the fallen barbed wire from the fence
that used to keep the pigs in.

My mother would say—
"look at this pig pen,"
referring to our bedroom
strewn with picture books
and naked dolls.
I didn't know it meant anything
but the product of our fun.

Had my mother spent time in or near pig pens?
I don't think so.
This sentence was passed down,
tongue to tongue,
mother to daughter.
Or was it her father
who was intimate with the homes of boars?

"It's as thin as a mosquito hide
stretched over a barrel,"
I overheard my grandfather say.

I wish I knew what he was describing.
It could only have been
the hair of an angel.
What else could be that fine?

Yet I always think of the paper
they used to sell
for sending things air mail—
translucent, strong as leather
to make it across oceans.
Does anyone care about
the weight of letters anymore?

My mother still asks if Bernie ever received
the birthday card she sent to me in Ecuador
two years ago, in care of him.
Last week she implored me to ask him again:
Did it arrive?
What has become of that card
she went to such trouble to select
and the $10 bill she stuck inside?

And while we're at it,
who in the Indian post office
ate those cookies she baked for me that Christmas
from my grandmother's recipe
sent to a remote village
halfway around the world
so I'd have my favorites — peanut butter drops,
rolled in sugar and topped with a chocolate star?

I loved them as a child.
Now? Impossibly rich and sweet.
And yet, if those cookies ever arrive,
I will eat them as prasad
invoking something precious
that can never be lost.

THIS CHANGES EVERYTHING

Loja, Ecuador

White colonial-era churches
stand like fortresses
while the rainforest chokes them back
and a woman relaxes
in her hammock, a spider monkey
between naked breasts.

Meanwhile, I walk the streets
amidst the blend of Spanish formality,
factory-made sparkle,
and the black cloth of the Saraguros
(indigenous to Peru,
pushed here in the 1500s by conquistadors).

The locals belong to something,
or pretend to, for this life.
But I am a visitor—
the one who stays at guest houses
that cater to the foreigner.
I am not allowed a culture.

Not this time.

In the Galapagos,
the plants came by mistake,
the seed of a flower stuck in a feather.

Just add time and you get a world
unlike all the others—
at least on the surface.

All places, all peoples,
come together from somewhere else.
We are made of one another.
This blending—
does it have to be a tragedy?

I used to think so.
But then the psychic stopped me,
anxious. My grandmother
had a message from the other side
where the ancestors live:
"It's a love story."

My grandmother, torn from her family
as a small girl, locked in a government
boarding school, forced to choose
one side of her tribe—
French or Menominee. She couldn't.
Left the reservation. Hid her blending.

With all that sorrow
still she says:
"It's a love story."

This changes everything.

BITTEN

Under thick skin,
grown to withstand wandering this world
with its guilty shadows
melting
in the shack where the fire won't light—

I am tender, a little crazy,
shackled with the heart
that wants heaven more than wisdom.

Hidden underneath:
the frightened spirit of the dark
just bitten by the light.

NO CURE

Himalayan Mountains, India

Barefoot on the cold ground
the monks in their red robes.
A heavy mist cloaks their shoulders
and the traditional naked arm—
willing to expand their comfort range
and with it, their compassion.

Too in love with comfort,
the wild nature starts to doze
and becomes a restless longing.
Blankets won't shield us
from the cold ground of being—
a tundra spreading with no relief.

Drop resistance
and we're skating,
laughing at numb fingers,
in love with the elements.

Let the wolves howl.
Put away the shotguns and the sheepskin.
There is no cure for hot and cold.

PERMISSION TO BE HUMAN

Andes Mountains, Ecuador

Permission to be human.
Have I been waiting for it?
Have we all been waiting?

As though some image
of the flawless or the mythic
were more worthy
than this humanness
with its squandered dreams,
empty pockets,
dirty socks,
bungled intentions.

Permission to rid myself
of any sense
that I might want to be
anywhere but here
on this earth
with the dog's howl
and that sad donkey.

NO MAP TO THIS TERRITORY

Now I'll stop pretending
that I know what I'm doing—
know anything about
what is happening here.

Steps alone make the trail
and leave only footprints.
No one has gone this way before.
No one has written a field guide

to my life.

Grasshoppers are
solitary creatures. They can only
jump forward, not backward
or sideways. In many cultures, they are symbols of
wisdom, good luck, abudance, leaps of faith and forward
momentum. Yet under conditions of sporadic rain fall, some
species undergo a Jekyll-to-Hyde transformation and become
swarming locusts. In Imperial China, grasshoppers were prized
for their songs and kept as pets believed to house the souls of
ancestors. This practice was forbidden during the cultural
revolution but is being revived and you can now find stalls
selling grasshoppers, along with cages designed to amplify their
songs, in Beijng markets.

acknowledgments

Special thanks to the Aya's Rivers flow fund for a gift supporting my six-month retreat in a small adobe cabin in the Andes mountains of Ecuador the winter of 2011. A number of these poems were born from that forest and the drone from the river that pervaded my time there—including the title poem. An additional gift from Hunter Reynolds allowed me a serendipitous retreat in 2012 at a guest house called "My Mum Home" in Chang Mai, Thailand, which continued in Ken Smith's shrine room in Bangkok, and then at Sri Nadi Homestay in Ubud, Bali, where I brought this book near to its final form amidst gamelon music, rooster symphonies and the mewing of newborn kittens.

A DEEP BOW TO LUIS RODRIGUEZ for his courageous inspiration, and to Hunter Reynolds, Tesa Silvestre, Nina Schnall, Satya Marga, Sarah Stone, Judy Woodburn, Coleen and Duane Elgin, Annik Brunet, Ken Farber, Felicia Lueger, my mother, and all who have engaged with my public writings such that I was encouraged to share further. Special thanks to Hal and Dana Farber for generously sharing their home, making possible my yearly visits to California throughout this long retreat time. And much gratitude to Lama Palden, Bokar Rinpoche, Leslie Gray, Kamalakar Mishra and Andrew Harvey for their inspiration and personal spiritual guidance as I've made my path by walking it.

MANY OF THESE POEMS were begun as freewrites done in Writing from the Soul circles (writingfromthesoul.net). Thanks to all the writers who have played with me in those circles, and to the sensitive, gutsy writers I've mentored individually. I hope this book inspires you to make one of your own.

THE FOLLOWING POEMS FIRST APPEARED in slightly different forms in the chapbook *Where the Buddhas Lay Their Eggs*, 2010, Flamingseed Press, and were written during my first stay in Ecuador and Costa Rica: "Willing to Bleed," "This Changes Everything," "Someone Put You There," "Wings," "So Tiny."

THE POEMS "Perfect Mudras" and "Here, Now" first appeared in the Wall of Miracles, an installation featuring poetry that honors aspects of the natural world, at Reed Hall/Wellness and Medical Centre, Streatham Campus, Exeter, UK. The installation was created by the poetry collective XEgesis.

THE QUOTE FROM NERUDA ON PAGE 11 is from the poem "Walking Around," which appeared in *Neruda & Vallejo: Selected Poems*, edited by Robert Bly, with translations by Robert Bly, John Knoepfle and James Wright. Boston: Beacon Press, 1971.

about the author

Jane Brunette has been writing since she could pick up a pen. Her primary focus in the past 15 years has been spiritual practice, and she has traveled widely, living simply in cultures where this is still possible in order to free her time and her mind for contemplation and retreat. She was born and raised in Chicago along with seven brothers and sisters by a French/ Menominee mother and Alsatian/Bavarian father, and through these roots, has a lineage connection to the Catholic mystical tradition and deep resonance with indigenous thought. A series of synchronicities led her to Tibetan Buddhism and in 2009, she was authorized as a Dharma teacher.

During her travels, she has taught meditation, spiritual practice and writing as a soul practice, as well as mentoring individuals in both writing and spiritual practice via Skype. In addition, she launched Flamingseed Press to publish books that grapple with the challenge of marrying spirit and earth. She holds an MA in Integral Counseling psychology from the California Institute for Integral Studies and an MA in Writing and Consciousness. Her writings can be found on the Huffington Post and at her websites: flamingseed.com and writingfromthesoul.net.

about flamingseed press

Flamingseed Press is a boundary-crossing experiment in publishing. The mission: To publish books that grapple with the challenge of marrying spirit to earth. They cross boundaries of culture and religion, generation and place, genre and paradigm, all with the intention of taking fast-changing times and challenging circumstances as inspiration to find more wise and soulful ways to live on our endangered planet, cultivating connection rather than division, love rather than fear. In addition to *Grasshopper Guru*, the press has thus far published *Brave New Prayers* by Hunter Reynolds, a collection of edgy, non-dual prayers that Rob Brezsny called "The best prayer book I've ever found—the holiest, rowdiest, truest and most intimately connected with the Divine Wow." A series of books on soul practices are currently under development. See flamingseedpress.com.

Some seeds only germinate in a forest fire. There are flowers in us that have been waiting for exactly these conditions.

35710840R00064

Made in the USA
Lexington, KY
22 September 2014